CABIN IN THE WOODS

CABIN IN THE WOODS

Written and Photographed by RALPH KYLLOE

Gibbs Smith, Publisher
TO ENRICH AND INSPIRE HUMANKIND
Salt Lake City | Charleston | Santa Fe | Santa Barbara

First Edition
11 10 09   5 4 3

PUBLISHED BY
Gibbs Smith, Publisher
P.O. Box 667
Layton, Utah 84041

Orders: 1.800.835.4993
www.gibbs-smith.com

DESIGNED BY Michelle Farinella Design
Printed and bound in China

 Library of Congress Control Number: 2007927417

ISBN 10: 1-4236-0200-5
ISBN 13: 978-1-4236-0200-2

For my wonderful wife Michele—you're the best!

Contents

Preface

This is my nineteenth book. Some people build homes or rustic furniture. Others act as legal counsel or invest other people's money. Still others practice medicine or drive trucks. I write books and make photographs. I love what I do: document and record the creative work of others more talented than I. And there are hundreds of thousands of others out there who do the same thing I do. Just walk into a major bookstore sometime and you'll realize that there really are millions of books on the market today. Nonetheless, I like to think I've had an influence, albeit small, on the field of rustic furniture and design. I see all kinds of homes and all kinds of rustic furniture. At my gallery in upstate New York, budding artists stop by just about every day (at least in the summer) to show me their latest creations. And a few times a week I receive portfolios from designers and architects who would love to see their work published. Frankly, I am incredibly encouraged each time I speak with any of these people. They have the drive to create something and the courage to show their work to others, which can be very scary if you don't have your head on straight. The potential for criticism or rejection is too much for some people. At the same time, I love speaking with entry-level people and, as an educator, take a bit of pride in realizing that they came to me for advice. Some novices go on to make really great furniture. I've had the pleasure of encouraging a few dozen individuals who have created careers for themselves in the rustic furniture business.

Architects are another matter. Usually a sophisticated group, a few have been annoyed when I've made slight suggestions that I felt would enhance their designs. Others have been grateful. I would have been an architect myself (I had four years of architectural design in high school) had I not found the math more than my simple mind could bear.

How I wound up in the rustic design business is a long story. My undergraduate degree is in photography and art history. I designed parks for my master's degree and also have a doctorate from Boston University. From there I went to the night school Harvard and completed a three-year program in business administration. While there I also studied astrophysics.

Thirty years ago I bought my first piece of antique rustic furniture. It was not what I had trained to do, but I fell in love with the antiques and art business. I'm my own boss and follow my own instincts. I love rustic stuff. I really do. I live in the Adirondack Park and have spent time in many of the great camps up here. About ten years ago I stumbled onto the creative geniuses in Bozeman, Montana. Although the historic camps of the East are exceptional, the architects and builders in the Bozeman area have brought rustic design to new heights. Their use of recycled materials is nothing less than profound. And their ability to create original rustic homes is awe-inspiring. I suspect there is something in the water out there that fosters great design and great artists.

Apart from all that, this book started out to be a book on small cabins. But as time went on, I kept finding really great homes that were larger than just small! And the homes were so gorgeous and inviting I had to include them in this book. So here they are! Each of the homes presented is more than just a pretty picture. Each has a passionate story behind it. Each is a bastion of joy and compassion. Each home is an object of art in itself. And each is a place where families come together and share the passions of play and bonding. The homes are not just structures; rather, they are living, breathing entities that help to make the world a better place.

Acknowledgments

As always, there are more people to thank than I can remember. But I'll do my best. Here goes!

My special thanks to Harry Howard and Nicole Bates at Yellowstone Traditions; architect Larry Pearson, Alyssa Ruffie, Katie Lineberger, Dennis Derham; Keith Anderson, and Josh Barr at LPAIA; architect Candace Miller; Jacque Spitler at Outlaw Design; Kam Faldapour; architect Kipp Halvorsen; Erica Hash; Jeff Sheldon; Bill Penniman; architect Jeff Thompson; Dick Beahrs; architect Owen Lawlor; Steve Boysol; Tony Cocca; Jill and Brian Gautie; John and Tina Keller; Chris Lohss; Peggy and Dennis Boyle; Josh Barr; Adam Britt; Greg Matthews and others too numerous to mention.

Also a special thanks to my editor, Madge Baird, for her unique ability to keep me focused when I'm up to my neck in projects. And to Christopher Robbins and Gibbs Smith at Gibbs Smith, Publisher, who both have the vision and courage to publish my books and many others that document the art of the West. And to my wife, Michele Kylloe; there is no way I would have accomplished what I have without her. My daughter, Lindsey Kylloe, has helped style many of my photographs and is an absolute asset to all of my efforts.

As a rule I never mention the names of the owners or where the homes are located. But to the owners of these great homes I express profound thanks! Thank you for your hospitality and for allowing me to include your homes in this book.

Introduction

It was still dark when I woke. I put on my robe and slippers and wandered down the hall to the shared bathroom at the Chico Hot Springs Lodge in Chico, Montana. The room was cheap and comfortable and I had stayed there many times over the years. Once back in my room, I dressed in my bathing suit and ambled down the old hallways to the outdoor pool. Water from the local hot springs poured into the structure about the size of an Olympic swimming pool and built in the 1930s. And although steam rose dramatically from the hot water, the stars in the sky shone brilliantly. I slipped into the half-filled pool and quickly immersed myself. The outside temperature was barely above freezing. I was the only one there. It was about 5 am. The hot water calmed me.

The pool itself is nothing more than a giant hot tub. In time a few more people wandered in and swam quietly in the soothing water. Dawn broke quietly and I could see the outlines of the mountains that surrounded the lodge. In time I returned to my room, shivering as I made my way. Other people were up now, and smells from the kitchen where chefs were busy preparing breakfast filled the halls.

In time I was dressed and wandered into the sitting room where I petted an old dog named Jasper who slept quietly, covered with an old blanket underneath a piano. Shortly after, I drove to an ancient cowboy bar near the lodge for breakfast. I drove slowly, as many deer hung near the edge of the road, and deer had been known to jump in front of moving vehicles. At the bar I had a single pancake and a glass of orange juice. Other patrons wandered in, sat near the pool table and smoked their cigarettes. One patron fed the juke-box and Patsy Cline sang a few country songs about heartache and misery. Oh, woe is me!

After breakfast I returned to my vehicle, dressed in my waders, assembled my fly-fishing gear and waited for my guide to appear. When he did, I followed him down to the access area, where we launched the boat. The Yellowstone River was quiet that day. There was no wind and we were the only fishermen on the water. I quite happily landed several brown trout on dry flies throughout the morning. They hit hard and jumped dramatically as I brought them close to the boat. They were quite happy to be released back to their watery homes after a few minutes of struggling. They belong in the water, not on the walls of trophy fishermen.

The river is lined with massive old-growth cottonwood trees. Deer are everywhere. Cows and sheep also wander near the river and drink the cold, clear water. Farms are everywhere present, as are fences.

Homes line the river as well. On many occasions, I've admired picturesque structures that appear to blend perfectly with the environment. They look like they have been there for many years. Being the consummate home viewer and a long-time student of regional architecture, I often gaze at homes when I should be paying attention to the trout that are rising.

On a ledge overlooking the river was an interesting structure that appeared to be a fire tower, but smaller. I took out my field glasses and eyed the building for a few minutes. In time, the guide calmly mentioned that we were approaching a set of rapids and asked me to sit down. After fishing that day, I wandered the roads on the east side of the river, looking for the home. But I didn't find it, and the structure passed from my memory.

A year later, Harry Howard from Yellowstone Traditions asked if I would like to see a few rustic structures on the Yellowstone River that his company had recently completed. I gladly accepted his offer. The following morning we visited the fire tower project I had seen a year earlier. It was a glorious structure.

The building started out as a small, single-room restack. In other words, an old historical log homestead building was found, disassembled and then reassembled (restacked) on a new site. The charm and character of old log cabins make them immensely desirable. The owners of the restack cabin immediately fell in love with their new structure and adorned it with old western items they had collected throughout the years. After the room was filled, they realized they wanted a bedroom; so another old building was found and attached to the first structure. In time, a third building was added and became a kitchen and dining area. Then two more old structures were attached to the ever-expanding building. These provided an exercise room, a recreation room complete with pool table and wet bar, and another area for the owners' collection of western antiques. And above it all was the fire tower, which gave the family extraordinary views of the Yellowstone River and the surrounding mountains.

I photographed the home over a two-day period in late summer. Harry Howard helped immensely with making the photos. Often when I photograph a kitchen or dining area, I place a wine bottle or coffee pot in an appropriate place to enhance the ambience and balance of the setting. On this particular day, I asked Harry to find a good-looking bottle of something. Moments later, he returned with a bottle of eighty-year-old scotch, which he artistically placed on the kitchen island. Of course, we needed a few glasses to complement the scene, so we placed two shot glasses near the bottle. And after looking at the scene through my camera, I made the decision to fill the glasses. Well, we did, and I believe that the photograph was greatly enhanced by the addition. Of course, we had to drink the scotch, as we did not want to waste what was obviously a quality product. I then decided to make another photograph of the kitchen at a different angle, so we again filled the glasses and made another photo. In truth, this went on for most of the afternoon and we made several great photos of the kitchen area. Harry is a bright, gregarious man, and our conversations throughout the day covered a wide range of topics. In time, Harry wound up taking an extended nap on the couch and I went on about my business. It was a grand day, one that I shall not forget. I just sincerely hope that the owner of the home does not realize that half a bottle of his expensive (and delicious) scotch is missing! And I must also add that when I received the photos back from the lab, I was relieved to see that the images I made that afternoon were all correctly exposed and in focus!

At any rate, the home in question was filled with extraordinary objects. Both functional and aesthetically pleasing, each piece in the extensive collection was handpicked over a period of many years. Good things take time, and homes, like collections, are never complete. But each new item comes with another story and another experience. The thrills of a flea market find or a hard-fought battle (i.e., expensive) at an auction are all experiences that bring meaning to each object and to each home.

Most of the homes I visit seem to be very organized, disciplined structures. They appear neat and orderly. But in the back of my mind, I'm fully aware that families live in these homes. They are not museums or stagnant receptacles of fiduciary responsibilities. It is in the homes I visit that families are grown.

Although cabins and camps and ranches are actual places, I often think of these words as verbs. They are active, ever-changing places that actively foster grand experiences that evolve into grand memories. And it is these memories that fire our passions and calm our souls.

When I was in the third and fourth grades, I lived with my family in the small town of Pardeville, Wisconsin. At that time my father was deathly ill, and we struggled, like many families, to make ends meet. But as an adult, my memories of that period in my life are softened by the thoughts of my daily summertime fishing activities. There were two lakes in town, and every day that the sun shined I made my way down to the lower lake with my friend Richard Deitman. As eight-year-olds, we would dig in the earth for worms and collect enough to last for another evening of fishing.

At around four in the afternoon, Richard and I made our way to the end of an old wooden pier that creaked and groaned as we settled in for a late afternoon of fishing. Neither of us had good gear. We would buy four hooks for a nickel and took care not to lose them. Our fishing poles were probably secondhand, and the reels often became stuck because we didn't have the proper lubrication to keep them finely tuned. For bobbers we both used small twigs tied to our lines. The fishing was extraordinary! Each evening we would catch fifty or so bluegills, sunfish or perch. We kept several of them each night, and I was proud to return home after sundown with dinner for the evening. But it was dusk that burns in my memory. The sun grew large and became brilliant orange. Ducks would often fly in front of the setting sun and honk their goodnights. The water became like glass, and we could hear a family of beavers from across the lake frolicking near the shore. As the sun dipped below the surface, the calls of an owl announced the beginning of his day. It was during that time that I figured out the very nature of black holes in space. I knew the sun was just a big fireball that would run out of fuel. And because it was spinning it had to compress, just like a whirlpool in my bathtub. It had to shrink to nothing and then disappear, I thought to myself. I called these thoughts "space pools," and when I mentioned them to my teacher during the school season, she didn't know what I was talking about. These, I think today, were strange thoughts for an eight-year-old kid in Wisconsin. But it was the peace and beauty of the evening and the cool air that I remember.

I always woke early in the morning. After breakfast I made my way down to the public beach where I learned to swim. By the middle of the summer, I was strong enough to swim out to the raft and spend the rest of the afternoon jumping off the diving board with dozens of other carefree kids. Around three in the afternoon, I returned home, picked up my fishing pole and made my way to the lake for another evening of grand thoughts and fishing.

Years later and back in Chicago, I joined the local Boys Club and traveled with many other inner-city kids to different camps. It was there where I enjoyed campfires and camp songs and marshmallows, ghost stories, canoe trips and hot dogs. In time I became a counselor at different camps around the country and continued my love affair with cabins and camps and the entire vacation experience. It's memories of these experiences that bring meaning to my life. And it's memories such as these that each of us associate with the cabins, lodges, resorts and ranches that we love. These are the places that allow us to discover who we are. We feel safe and carefree at camp. These are places of peace and comfort. This is where strong individuals and strong families are built and sustained. The fun and joy of the cabin is nothing less than hypnotic. And it is these memories that I'll take into my very old age.

Rocky Mountain Arts and Crafts Home

Resting on the eastern slopes of the northern Rocky Mountains is a contemporary Arts and Crafts home. Designed by architect Larry Pearson, the home blends well with the local rock formations and stands of mature pine trees. Modeled after and influenced by the architecture of the Arts and Crafts period of the early 1900s, the home was completed with aged, recycled materials. The stonework was completed by Sandoval Masonry of Bozeman, Montana. Josh Barr served as project manager for the construction of the home, and the owners were the decorators.

The exterior of the home is complete with cedar shake shingles and locally found recycled timbers. The siding is recycled fir. Angel Sandoval of Sandoval Masonry used Montana gold and bronze rock for the columns and chimney system. The tapered columns, dormers and overhangs are classic Arts and Crafts elements.

The dining room offers a built-in fireplace complete with classic green tiles. The floors throughout are reclaimed oak. Mica shades cover the lights on the chandelier.

The kitchen stove boasts a copper hood. Softly colored green and tan tiles cover the walls below the mahogany cabinets. A butcher block counter-top covers the island, which also offers a wet sink. The countertops below the cabinets are dark marble. Simple, single hanging lights add to the calm elegance of the home.

The main entry door to the home was made from mahogany. The homeowner, an accomplished artist, created the stained glass window for the door. The form of the door suggests a California Greene and Greene influence.

The downstairs bedroom offers a full-size antique iron bed complete with Native American textiles and leather throw pillows. Air circulated by the ceiling fan and the red walls add life and energy to the setting.

The owners decorated the home themselves. A string of pumpkin lanterns adorning the fireplace mantel announce an impending party.

Columns of mahogany and fir are sentinels in the entryway to the living room. Recycled beams add texture, while recycled oak floors bring a sense of warmth.

An oversized sofa covered in soft green fabric and large leather armchairs make the living room inviting. The coffee table was made from locally found barn boards.

Paradise Valley Fire Tower

The building is a compilation of four different historical structures. Most of the roof system is covered with shake shingles. The light-colored section of the building is a recent addition.

Several comments regarding this home are included in the introduction to this book. Charming in every way, the home is actually four old log homesteads that were disassembled from various locations around Montana and reassembled together on their present site. The home started as a single room. As time passed, the owners sought to expand the building; so additions were made that resulted in the living room, kitchen, bedroom and game room. Finally the fire tower was added. The homeowners did the decorating as they went along. Bill Penniman and the creative folks at Yellowstone Traditions served as architects. The building was constructed by Yellowstone Traditions. Brett Evje of Yellowstone Rock Works and Rod Cranford of North Fork Stone Works were the masons.

This room, with an antique door leading
to the outside, houses part of an extensive
collection of western rustic memorabilia.
An old beaver skin coat hangs on the wall
and buffalo hide chaps rest on the antique
table. Other accessories such as lariats and
gloves complement the setting.

A massive grizzly bear paw complete
with claws stands guard in the fire tower.

The kitchen area contains custom-made cabinets of recycled materials and a contemporary "old-fashioned" stove. The cabinet doors are covered with screen to prevent flies from attacking the food.

Another view of the custom kitchen island and
cabinets made of recycled materials.

The bedroom offers this folk art rocker (probably from Pennsylvania) and a 1920s floor lamp with hide shade.

The bedroom offers this 1920s full-size brass bed covered with country quilts and textiles.

The highest viewing room of the fire tower, complete with country chairs and table to enjoy your lunch, reveals dramatic views of the Yellowstone River. A grizzly bear in upright stance guards the room.

The fire tower's subtle roofline reflects the silhouette of the mountain ranges in the distance.

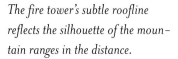

One of several collection rooms hosting western antiques, this one displays saddles and traps.

The living room, the first to have been restacked on the site, is home to an extensive collection of antique spurs. Oversized leather couch and armchairs serve as seating, where one can enjoy the warmth of a roaring fire. The lengthy coffee table was created from recycled pine.

Another room is complete with a pool table, kept
company by an original shoe shine platform with
matching armchairs. A stuffed billy goat guards the
doorway and an authentic Navajo rug rests on the floor.

The door, made from recycled barn beams, and its heavy hinges were created by the folks at Yellowstone Traditions.

An exterior sectional view of two of the doors shows fine craftsmanship and consistency in design. The colors of the locally quarried rock and the recycled timbers blend naturally together.

A dramatic vista of the Yellowstone River from the balcony. The railings were created from dead-standing lodgepole pine trees.

The exposed balcony is quite suitable for viewing the mountains and keeping a lookout over the valley. Harsh storms often sweep through here, remind visitors of the strength inherent in nature.

Grizzly bears, deer, wolves, antelope,
moose and bison are just some of the
frequent visitors to the surrounding valley.

A view of the roof system shows extensive rock work throughout the building. One section of the roof is covered with sod and local wild grasses that grow prolifically.

A detail section of the building shows the fusion of locally quarried rocks and historic timbers. Two different companies, *Yellowstone Rockworks* and *North Fork Stone Works*, provided masons for the project.

Paradise Valley Cabin

Just down the road apiece from the Fire Tower sits the Paradise Valley cabin. The land purchase included existing historical buildings. Architect Bill Penniman of Penn Co Design and Harry Howard of Yellowstone Traditions served as architects for the project. Yellowstone Traditions restored the buildings. The mason was Rod Cranford.

Small in size, the home is a weekend vacation retreat with great mountain views. A traditional overhanging porch has room enough for four rocking chairs. Wild animals visit the cabin on a daily basis.

As in many homes, the fireplace is the
centerpiece here. An old barn beam serves
as a mantel. A set of Native American
drums sits near the recycled wood cabinet.
An oversized leather couch invites guests to
relax after a hard day of fly-fishing.

Outside the front door sits this handmade one-door, one-drawer cabinet that acts as a stand for a coffee pot.

The kitchen area, although small, offers enough space to prepare gourmet meals. Granite covers the countertops. The range hood is hand forged.

The dining area is complete with a small table and six hickory chairs, plus plenty of wall hooks to hang jackets and outdoor gear.

Another corner of the living room has a cabinet to store one's books and papers as well as a handmade stick rocker and Native American textiles.

The single bedroom has a generously proportioned bed and geometric-patterned covering.

Black Butte Ranch

Blending with the environment, a secondary cabin of traditional rustic design offers bedrooms and complete living quarters. The golden colors of fall are the perfect complement to the rustic setting.

We left town at around nine a.m. and arrived at the ranch an hour and a half later. I could never find the site again if my life depended on it. Once off the highway, the dusty gravel road required that we drive about five miles per hour. First a barn appeared, then a small cabin, then a flock of turkeys, and then two small stone cabins came into view. Located on the shores of the Boulder River, a blue-ribbon trout stream, eagles and ospreys fled from overhanging trees as I carefully wandered near a few deep pools to watch for signs of rising fish. Wildlife was every-where. Black Butte Ranch was not at all what I had expected. As we approached the complex, the barn contained typical garage doors no different from thousands of other barns. The entire complex, at first glance, was both unassuming and unpretentious. Then we went around to the rear of the barn and entered the building, and what grand design and craftsmanship were in store. The architect for the project was Jeff Shelden of Prairie Wind Architecture. After significant consideration, the owners wanted something quite different from the many "trophy cabins" that are popular today. Ultimately, a traditional "line camp and cabins" seemed appropriate for the setting. Yellowstone Traditions served as general contractor, while masonry duties were shared by three different companies, including Yellowstone Rockworks, Hardrock Masonry and North Fork Stone Works. Hilary Heminway was the interior designer.

The rear of the "barn" proved to be far more visually interesting than the side that first appeared on the approach to the ranch. The exterior lines of the building reflect a Scandinavian influence. A boot-jack fence lines the property. The barn, today, is affectionately known as "Yonder."

Using locally found stones, masons and carpenters created these two small structures on the property. The house on the left serves as a guest cabin and the building on the right houses the power plant and other utilities.

The geometric design of the cabins is enhanced by the linear design of the door and sconce.

The living room of the guest cabin offers traditional armchairs and sofas. The stones for the fireplace were acquired from the local river. An elk head over the fireplace enjoys the company of the many guests that stay in the cabin. Hilary Heminway was the interior designer for the complex.

An overview of the living room shows a dining table with western-style side chairs. The mantel is a standing dead lodgepole pine tree sawn in half. The built-in bookcases hold leather-bound books and table games. The sofa was hand stitched.

The kitchen in the guest cabin offers a bar-type setting complete with three western-style bar stools for a quick meal. The countertops contain marble insets. The range hood, area behind the countertops and refrigerator facade are lined with textured copper. The simple kitchen cabinet drawer pulls are reminiscent of the 1920s. Mica shades take their place on the three suspended lights..

The entry to the main guest
cabin offers a sofa table made
from recycled barn beams.
The intricate leather mirror
was created by artist Chris
Chapman. Hooks on the wall
provide places to hang coats,
cowboy hats and other stuff.

Soft-toned textiles were used to complement the colors of buildings. This queen bed made from locally found recycled materials offers throw pillows and a down comforter—absolute musts for cold mountain nights.

This bed was created by rustic artist Lester Santos of Cody, Wyoming.

Another kids' room offers a bunk bed made from recycled barn beams. Drawers in the base of the bed provide convenient storage for visitors. The wilderness-themed throw rug keeps feet warm on cold mornings.

The kids' room in the main building contains rustic bunk beds and enough toys to keep any child quite happy.

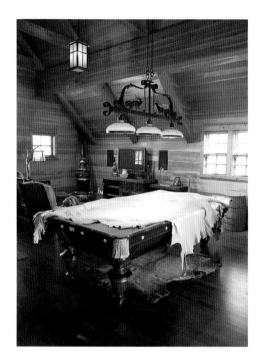

In a corner of the recreation room are a pool table (presently covered with an elk hide), a wood stove and a number of comfortable armchairs for TV watching when the fish aren't biting.

The upstairs of the ranch "barn" is the gathering and recreation room, where an elaborate full wet bar is readily put to use. A bison hide rests on the recycled pine floor and an elk mount guards the room. Created in post and beam style, the room is lighted with hanging Arts and Crafts–style lanterns.

The downstairs meeting room in "Yonder" contains a fly-tiers desk boasting every element needed to tie flies. The room also holds a wood stove, several designer armchairs, taxidermy and a massive safe that doubles as a secure gun cabinet.

This tall combination desk and cabinet was made by the cabinetmakers at Yellowstone Traditions. Lodgepole pine is the material.

The small guest cabin on the property contains another lodgepole cabinet that is used to display accessories and provide storage.

A flock of wild turkeys attended our visit and seemed annoyed when I wanted to photograph building exteriors.

All homes need a "rest
room." Yet another corner
of the gathering room offers
this unique rest room
designed in the style of
a traditional outhouse.

White Fish Hills

The entire compound encompasses twenty acres, six structures, a well-stocked trout pond with a beach and swimming hole, and a corral and structure for the horses. Wildlife was ever-present, and a friendly pair of barnyard cats seemed to follow us wherever we went!

I had been in Cody, Wyoming, in late September. From there I flew to Alaska for a week of trout fishing. The return trip to Bozeman, Montana, was a near disaster. All of my flights were late taking off and I missed all of my connections. It was nearly twenty hours of airport hot dogs, waiting rooms and crowded planes. I hadn't slept and my bones ached. In Bozeman, architect Jeff Thompson greeted me when I got off the plane. I just wanted to get a hotel room and pass out. But Jeff, in a very polite way, insisted that I travel with him to see a recently completed project that he had worked on with Yellowstone Traditions and architect Larry Pearson. Being an accommodating individual, I agreed to see the home and loaded my gear in his SUV. He failed to mention that the site was a five-hour drive north. So off we went. I told my stories and he told his and we actually got along very well. Jeff is an affable young man who enjoys riding his mountain bike as much as he does designing homes. Two hours into the trip I passed out and slept for three hours. I woke up near Glacier National Park. For lunch I had a can of red Powerade and a package of Twizzlers. In time Jeff pulled off the main road, stopped, and entered a code on a key pad in front of a large iron gate. The key pad beeped and an iron gate slowly opened. Deer and wild turkeys were everywhere. A winding road led us first to a grand home and then to another and another. We stopped in front of the first house, took our luggage from the car and entered the home. Designed by architect Larry Pearson and constructed by Yellowstone Traditions, the guesthouse, as it is called, is 1,800 square feet of rustic living space. The attached sunroom, which overlooks the trout pond, is considered by the owners to be the finest room in the compound. Pearson also created the master plan for the entire compound.

The Guesthouse

The guesthouse, designed by Larry Pearson, offers 1,800 square feet of living space including three bedrooms, a kitchen and dining area, and an attached sunroom. The building offers shake shingles, vertical logs under the eaves and shiplap boards on the exterior.

The custom kitchen cabinets made with aged barn boards offer significant workspace. The countertops are black granite. Wainscoting covers the front of the cabinets and is painted turquoise. A cast-iron old-style gas stove provides a flame to heat hot chocolate on cool evenings. And old soapstone sink covered with hammered copper serves as a place to clean dirty dishes and dirty hands. The top of the kitchen island is covered with recycled fir.

*A six-foot refectory table
and six Spanish-influenced
dining chairs offer dining
space for guests. A cylinder
roll-top cabinet provides
storage space for kitchen
utensils and other necessities.
The chandelier is an old
horse harness holding
three lanterns.*

Oversized armchairs covered with dark textured leather serve as seating just off the kitchen. Pots of cut wildflowers bring nature indoors. The floor is recycled fir.

The downstairs master bath offers a soak in a claw-foot tub or a nice hot shower. Candles and floral arrangements add ambiance to the room, and the only thing you'll see out the windows are wild turkeys or deer! The vanity is an antique sideboard. Metal tiles cover the ceiling.

The living room, which sits directly under an exposed balcony, offers an upholstered sofa, coffee table and floral design rug for the enjoyment of the visitors. The exposed rafters in the home, made of dead standing logs, bring character to the setting.

The floor to ceiling tapered fireplace adds definite drama to the room. The mantel provides display area for Native American baskets, family photos and other collectibles. A traditional western painting with limited palette hangs over the fireplace.

The downstairs bedroom contains this classic Southwestern king-size bed. The textured wall behind the headboard is painted mustard yellow. Heavy textiles keep visitors warm at night.

The exposed second-floor balcony offers traditional Arts and Crafts windows in the dormers and three comfortable beds with individual floor lamps. The pair of beds with red covers appear to be Spanish in origin.

The sunroom is described as the best room in the complex. Offering comfortable wicker furniture, a turn-of-the-century rocker and a chess set, the room is ideal for watching the sun set when the mosquitoes are biting!

The back door, custom made by Yellowstone Traditions, seems to be used the most, as it leads directly to the beach!

The Lodge

Designed by architect Jeff Thompson, the buildings were, nonetheless, a fusion of ideas between the owner, superintendent Michael Jones of Yellowstone Traditions and the architect. Cheryl Griffin was closely involved in the interior design of the home. Mark Johnson of Majestic Mountain Landscaping expertly completed the landscaping for the entire project.

Offering more than 4,500 square feet of living space, the lodge includes three bedrooms, office, kitchen, dining room, bar, wine cellar and several baths. The exterior of the home wears stained horizontal lap siding and vertical four-inch half-round logs under the gable ends and eaves. The roof is shake shingle.

Seen from across the pond, the home is a picture of tranquility. The exquisitely designed compound took two years to complete.

Hanging pots of flowers and porch chairs add character and charm to the front of the lodge.

The great room in the lodge has layer after layer of texture and
composition. Four massive armchairs rest in front of the fireplace.
A massive stone wall separates the great hall from the bedrooms
and office. The room is subtly lighted with hanging cylinder lights.
A recessed section adds depth to the fireplace. Native American
carpets hang from the banisters of the balcony.

Instead of a couch, four massive armchairs create a seating arrangement in front of the fireplace. The rich golden hue in the carpet picks up the coloring of the walls. The use of dead standing logs provides drama and character to the setting.

The rich tapestry fabric on the chairs and coffee table brings distinction to the home. The armchairs are Spanish in origin. The fireplace design creates interesting shelves and alcoves.

A massive textured sofa and complementary throw pillows grace the living room. The liberal use of floral arrangements brings nature indoors. A variety of Native American artifacts serve as accessories throughout.

Down a secret passage through the wet bar is a set of stairs leading to the wine cellar, which holds a minimum of three hundred bottles of vintage wine! The table and four chairs, as well as the chandelier, are antiques.

A full wet bar neatly tucked behind the fireplace is complete with coolers and ice makers.

The geometric patterns in the staircase are a good complement to the design of the room. The flooring is recycled pine. A rich brown fabric on the side chairs extends the color-rich tones of the floor. And the dial telephone really works!

*The dining room hosts an
antique Caucasian carpet and
eight-foot trestle table with
eight matching dining chairs.*

The kitchen boasts custom built-in cabinetry.
Glass-front upper cabinets make it easier to
find things. Decorative tiles cover the walls
below the hood and under the cabinets.
A large refrigerator is camouflaged behind
cabinet doors. Marble tops the island, and
single-cone chandeliers made of tin light
the food preparation area.

An antique French cabinet embellished with original paintings acts as a server in the dining area. The antique dining table is made of elm.

Marble covers the countertops, while an industrial Viking range provides a flame to cook the meals. Simple hardware reminiscent of the 1920s serves as door/drawer pulls on the cabinets. Hammered-copper insets complete the range hood.

The carriage house also contains a small kitchen with sink, microwave and built-in cooler. The cabinets were made from recycled boards.

Down a long hallway and isolated from the main part of the home is a small office where the owner can keep tabs on his many business interests.

The second floor offers two complete bedrooms neatly tucked under the eaves. Each bedroom includes a private bath and has a colorful textile covering the bed.

*The master bedroom is complete with
a TV that rises out of the footboard!
The corner fireplace and candles
lend intimacy.*

Attached to the main lodge via a breezeway is a carriage house that provides both parking for a few classic vehicles and an upstairs apartment for extra guests. Consistent in design with the main lodge, the building has vertical logs under the gable ends, a stone entryway and more than 1,600 square feet of usable space.

The master bath includes his-and-her hammered-copper sinks in the custom vanity. Matching mirrors complete the ensemble. A full shower is just around the corner.

The entranceway to the carriage house was created from locally found stones that were flat stacked.

*The upstairs apartment contains
a dramatic iron bed.*

Outdoor Gazebo

The owner requested a freestanding exterior space to entertain. Two months later the gazebo was complete. Perhaps the most "laid back" structure in the compound, the building has vertical timbers and a stone wall supporting the back. Located near the putting green, it blends perfectly with the environment.

Cozy wicker armchairs, footstools and sofas make comfortable seating. The putting green and pitching field for golf lovers can be seen in the background.

The building offers a complete wet bar, gas-fired grill (we cooked buffalo steaks during my stay) and coolers large enough to provide cold beverages to satisfy a few busloads of thirsty people! The back windows, which boast 9 mm bullet holes, were found in a Montana basement.

Evening brings a roaring fire, refreshments and a chance to relax and tell stories of the day. The locked cabinet in the background houses a huge flat-screen TV; the architect and I watched the latest James Bond movie before retiring for the night.

The Pond Shack

Across the pond sits a small cabin that appears to have been on the site since Buffalo Bill Cody wandered the West. Affectionately known as the "Pond Shack," the building is 392 square feet of living and play space. The roof was created from cold rolled steel. An outer layer of the roof rusts almost immediately, but the inner layers of the material remain intact and last for many years.

A "designer" barn on the large property contains workshops and room for equipment and other vehicles. An old log structure found a hundred miles from the compound was dismantled and reassembled as the main barn structure. Two cats that claim it as home happily go about their days chasing mice and squirrels. A boot-jack fence corrals several horses.

The interior of the "shack" is complete with a pair of twin bunk beds, rustic game/dining table, a few armchairs and plenty of toys and board games.

The bathroom vanity in the Pond Shack was created from an antique cart, while the sink is an old water bucket.

Domaille Residence at Yellowstone Club

I had seen the home under construction for more than two years. The site was 11,000 feet above sea level, and I had been stuck in the driveway more than once battling several feet of snow typical at that elevation. Designed by architect Candace Miller of Livingston, Montana, the home offers 7,000 square feet of living space. Two master suites, a guest bedroom and bunkroom, kitchen, dining room, study, four full baths, three powder rooms, two interior fireplaces and one exterior fireplace offer the owners and their guests comfortable living after a day of skiing or golf. From the road (it's in a guarded, gated community), the building first appears unassuming. But the grandeur of the home is exposed as one ventures down the driveway. Artfully constructed by the talented craftsmen at Lohss Construction, the home is a fusion of recycled and restacked homestead cabins boasting exceptional stonework completed by Evje Masons. The interior design was completed by Debra Schull at Design Associates.

The front of the home offers a fusion of recycled timbers and
creative stonework. Homes such as this are actually "stick
built," meaning the home is traditionally constructed with
studs and beams. The electrical wiring, insulation and
plumbing are then hidden in the walls. The recycled timbers
are split down the middle and artfully applied to both the
interior and exterior of the building. A home constructed in
this fashion becomes energy efficient. The roof of the building
is cedar shake shingles. The exposed rafters on the exterior
of the building add visual motion to the form of the structure.
Chinking, a flexible, gluelike material, is applied
between the logs to further weatherproof the structure.
Considerable landscaping, including the placement of huge
boulders around the property, completes the setting.

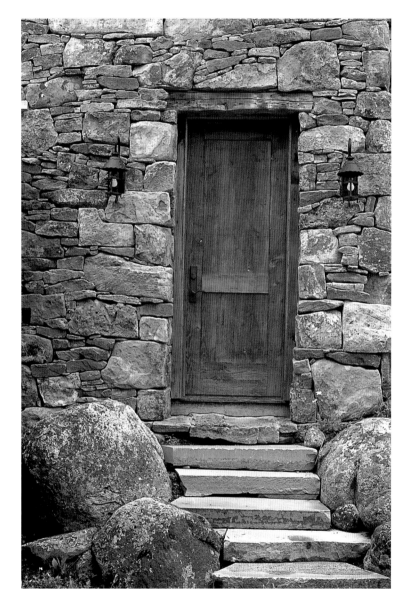

Simple iron sconces placed tastefully around the exterior add subtle light on dark evenings.

Custom-made doors and stone staircases help the home blend with its environment.

The living room offers huge floor-to-ceiling
windows from which one can enjoy the dramatic
mountain views. The mantel for the fireplace
was created from a recycled barn beam. The
antique coffee table is English, and the armchair
is covered with dark, textured leather. A soft
green fabric covers the backs of two sofas, and
the carpet is Caucasian.

Another view of the living area shows the high ceilings made with recycled rafters and a four-tier chandelier made from iron and elk antlers. An antique English sideboard acts as a sofa table and storage area behind the couch. A square, iron-legged table in rustic motif serves as a side table between the couches.

A different angle of the living room demonstrates the open aspects of the home and shows an upstairs balcony lounge area, complete with armchairs and accessories.

Creative use of available materials adds interest and uniqueness to the setting.

The rear of the home offers an extensive open-air patio area and a tall fireplace for roasting hot dogs and marshmallows.

A massive dining table surrounded by
eight large dining chairs with leather seats
and backs completes the dining room. A
simple eight-light chandelier illuminates
the dining area.

A detail photo of the dining room
armchair and an afternoon wine setting,
complete with a good Bordeaux and
snacks, provides a glimpse of the
"atmosphere" at the home.

The food preparation area offers a breakfast counter and four bar stools covered with rich blue fabric. The counter-top is covered with recycled barn boards. The kitchen island, complete with a wet sink, and related countertops are covered with granite slabs. The refrigerator and freezer are recessed behind wooden doors. Textured tiles cover the wall below the cupboards. The simple hanging light is diffused by a hide shade embellished with pinecone motif. The floor is made of recycled, rough-cut pine boards.

Just off the living room is a passageway sitting area that offers floor-to-ceiling built-in bookcases, a desk and two highly textured leather armchairs. Tastefully arranged organic materials add form to the setting and complement the area.

This master bath has custom built-in cabinets, a high-drama hammered-copper bathtub, marble bowls as sinks and Japanese-style faucets for the tub and sinks!

A vaulted ceiling plus deep windows make the master bedroom feel spacious. A twelve-light, two-tiered iron chandelier is an understated centerpiece. Two arm-chairs make this a comfortable sitting room as well.

This second-floor bedroom offers a king-size, bark-on rustic bed complete with floral bed coverings that complement the carpet. The walls have been painted a soft pastel color to accent the ancient ceiling beams. The room also offers a pair of upholstered armchairs and a custom tall cabinet that serves as an armoire. It is lit with a simple three-light iron chandelier and strategically placed lamps.

The bunk room is complete with a pair of single-over-double bunk beds made of hickory wood. The beds are covered with warm, colored textiles that complement the vintage materials used to construct the home.

Rock Creek Camp

The project aimed to capture the bucolic feel of the historic Montana landscape. Just like the early pioneers, the owners selected a site near water that offered cool summer breezes. The roof, in traditional low-slung, trapper's cabin design, is covered with shake shingles. The home is a traditional restack of old, historic materials.

From Cody, Wyoming, you travel north over the Chief Joseph Highway toward Red Lodge, Montana. If heights scare you, take a different route. The Bear Tooth Pass over the Absaroka Range is a white-knuckle drive that offers more beauty than the average person can comprehend. Once your heart settles and your blood pressure goes down, you'll enjoy rolling hills, as well as herds of elk, deer and an occasional moose. In time, you'll find Rock Creek, a smaller stream that native rainbow trout call their home. Upstream is Rock Creek Camp. Designed by architect Kipp Halvorsen of Faure Halvorsen Architects, the home is a model of rustic simplicity and elegant taste. T & M Construction built the home and Erica Hash of Kibler and Kirsch designed its interior.

Old oil lanterns serve as sconces and accent the rustic nature of the home. The custom doors are a statement of simplicity.

The form of the home is complemented with simple, intersecting lines. The main entryway and adjoining hallway, made of stone, are covered with a small shed roof.

A tall, tapered chimney system highlights the exterior of the home.

The back porch offers a secluded, covered area for outdoor meals.

The simple kitchen offers an island with a marble top and hickory chairs. Simple tin pulls adorn the cabinets.

The home, created and designed as an open setting, offers a kitchen, dining room and living room. The living room contains a trestle table with six hickory chairs. The highly figured logs and the recycled pine floor add character to the room.

The king–size bed has lively textiles and a bed covering that add energy to the room. An easy chair and ottoman allow for a quiet moment after a hard day's fishing.

The living room is casual and unpretentious:
the roaring fire begs visitors to relax, the
open-air bookshelves provide space to
display collectibles and family heirlooms,
and a small television offers passive enter-
tainment on cold evenings.

A large barn also graces the setting. A generous
open area in the loft serves as a recreation site for
the family, while the lower area houses vehicles,
a workshop and horse stalls.

The entryway to the home includes a full bathroom, hooks for coats and a bench to change shoes, or display floral arrangements.

The bathroom includes a vanity with wood slab top and antique-style sink.

OO Ranch

Overlooking prairies, trout ponds and mountains (not shown) this small, unassuming cabin sits on a rolling hill in the path of an approaching storm.

Overlooking a dramatic vista of prairies and mountains, this small cabin was designed by architect Candace Tillotson-Miller as a guest home for a couple to occupy while their main house was designed and constructed. The home sits low to the ground and offers a low-slung shed roof over half of the building. The roof is covered with cold-rolled steel, which quickly acquires an aged appearance once installed. The capped chimney complements the simple lines of the building. The home offers 2,200 square feet of living space. Yellowstone Traditions constructed the building and Jamie Livingston of Hardrock Masonry completed the stonework. Debra Schull of Design Associates was the interior designer for the project.

The small, comfortable living room offers a designer selection of seating to help occupants enjoy the dramatic fireplace. A custom-made country table in Arts and Crafts style serves as a dining table. The tall windows on the right allow for views of the mountains, while the left windows overlook a rolling prairie.

The entrance is through a screened porch, where a rustic stick table and four chairs are often occupied in the warm months during dinnertime. A dramatic Native American rug lies under the table. The exposed studs and rafters add to the rustic ambiance of the home. A porch swing with an upholstered cushion sits in a corner of the room.

The bedroom offers a massive, king-size, four-poster bed. Two lights covered with birch bark shades are suspended from the ceiling. A ceiling fan circulates air, while the windows are covered with simple drawstring rolling blinds.

The small kitchen is enhanced by vaulted ceilings and dramatic recycled beams. An antique Pennyan boat fits nicely on a recessed shelf. The room is illuminated by four chandeliers with hide shades. The countertops of the island and workstations are covered with tin. The floors are covered with recycled barn boards.

Copper Cabin

This extraordinary cabin is actually a modified restack. The original cabin, constructed in the 1880s, was found in Montana's Flat Head Valley.

It is the sister building to the Trading Post Cabin, a national historic landmark that stands today in St. Ignatius, Montana. The cabin was dismantled and reassembled by the creative folks at Chris Lohss Construction in Gallatin Gateway, Montana. It was greatly modified and altered by Chris Lohss to meet the needs of the client. Assembled and presently residing at 11,000 feet above sea level, its foundation had to be dug an additional eight feet below the surface because of loose soil conditions. The building sits on a steep slope, and if you're at all nervous about heights, don't have lunch on the back porch. The building as it stands offers 1,800 square feet of living space and is heated with an electric boiler and radiant heat. Andrew Varella of Set-in-Stone Masonry was the mason.

The living room offers a tapered fireplace surround. Antique western accessories complement the home. A moose head, which rests over the windows, guards the room. The window treatments are custom-made cowhide curtains.

The entry to the home is through this door, hand made of ancient recycled materials.

Overlooking a dramatic mountain range, Copper Cabin sits on the lee side of a mountain and is the perfect place to watch the storms roll in. One section of the roof is made of shake shingles and another section is covered with grass.

*The sofa is covered with buffalo hides
and adorned with the horns of
bighorn sheep. The coffee table is an
old steamer trunk and the lamp
shades are cowhide.*

The outside back porch overlooks a championship golf course in the valley below.

The main living room also includes a staircase that descends to a basement recreation room.

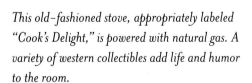

This old-fashioned stove, appropriately labeled "Cook's Delight," is powered with natural gas. A variety of western collectibles add life and humor to the room.

The cooking area includes custom cabinets, western-inspired dinnerware and old-fashioned appliances.

The opposite end of the great room includes a kitchen and dining area. The chandelier was created by Lester Santos. An upstairs balcony houses a bed, desk and easy chair. The floors throughout the building are recycled barn boards.

The upstairs loft includes a desk, easy chair and this brightly covered bed.

Hawk Eye Ranch

I've known rustic artist Lester Santos for many years, so when he mentioned that he had a house I should see, I did not hesitate. The occasion was the Western Design Conference in Cody, Wyoming, where I was presenting. In the afternoon, Lester, his wife and I, along with interior designer Chip Kalleen and furniture builder Reid Crosby, hopped into two vehicles and traveled for an hour and a half up the south fork of the Shoshone River. Frankly, it was a perilous drive. My vehicle wound up in a ditch (I was driving), and if there hadn't been four-wheel drive, I would never have gotten back on the road. In time, the dirt road narrowed and our driving slowed. The tall mountains closed in on us and the potholes, filled with water and ice, brought us almost to a standstill. Finally, we traveled down an obscure road, and there stood Hawk Eye Ranch. Built in the 1930s, the ranch is one of the oldest dude ranches in Wyoming and is now a private retreat.

Hawk Eye Ranch sits neatly in a valley surrounded by towering mountain peaks. Several buildings are on the property, including a great hall, horse barn and small residences for the owner and guests.

*The great hall, recently com-
pleted by Tom Quick
Construction, includes this
massive fireplace. The
chandeliers were created
by Peter Fillerup. Navajo
carpets cover the floor.
Rustic artist Lester Santos
constructed the furniture,
including the armchairs
and sofas.*

A sitting room off the main hall is complete with a medium-size grizzly bear and built-in bookcases.

The sitting room also offers a small fireplace and high-end armchairs in traditional western style by Lester Santos.

The antique pool table sits on a contemporary room-size Navajo carpet.

Lester Santos constructed the bar, whose countertops are covered with hammered copper. Peter Fillerup created the chandeliers and Darius Sasmauskaf made the bar stools. Here we get a clear view of the tin-covered ceiling.

*The ornate, round dining table
and matching side chairs were
constructed by Lester Santos.*

Resources

Interior Designers

Butterbrodt Design Associates,
Lisa Butterbrodt, ASID
1155 Camino Del Mar #445
Del Mar, CA 92014
858.792.5400

Carole Sisson Designs, ASID
117 E. Main Street
Bozeman, MT 59715
406.587.2600

Diana Beattie Interiors
1136 Fifth Ave.
NY, NY 10128
212.722.6226

Gallinger Trauner Design, Cheryl Gallinger
3785 S. Lake Creek Drive
Wilson, WY 83014
307.733.0902

Greenauer Design Group, Melissa Greenauer
PO Box 5963
Vail, CO 81658
970.926.1783

Hilary Heminway
140 Briarpatch Road
Stonington, CT 06378
860.535.3110

Lohr Design
Chip Kalleen
201 N. Illinois St., Ste. 1720
Indianapolis, Indiana 46204
317.237.5610
518.743.1148

Kibler & Kirch
101 North Broadway
Red Lodge, Montana 59068
406.446.2226 phone
406.446.2228 fax

Outlaw Design
Jacque Spitler
3947 Baxter Lane
Bozeman, MT 59718
406.624.0199
406.599.0837

WISE Associates, Heidi Weiskopf
23150 N. Pima Road #1E
Scottsdale, AZ 85255
602.625.9832

Architects

Candace Tillotson–Miller Architects
208 W. Park
PO Box 470
Livingston, MT 59047
406.222.7057

Dan Joseph
PO Box 4505
Bozeman, MT 59772
734.428.1900
800.800.3935

Jeff Thompson
220 S. Ninth Ave.
Bozeman, MT 59715
406.586.3553

Kipp Halvorsen
1425 West Main St., Ste. A
Bozeman MT 59715
406.587.1204

Larry Pearson AIA
PO Box 3666
Bozeman, MT 59715
406.587.1997

Prairie Wind Architecture
Jeff Shelden, AIA
206 West Boulevard
PO Box 626
Lewistown, MT 59457
406.538.2201

Urban Design Group
Peter Dominick
1621 18th St., Ste 200
Denver, CO 80802
303. 292.3388

Home Builders

Chris Lohss Construction
PO Box 556
Gallatin Gateway, MT 59730
406.763.9081

Green Farm/Lawlor LandUse
Owen Lawlor, Project Manager/Principal
612 Spring St.
Santa Cruz, CA 95060-2030
831.457.1331
831.212.8594

OSM
417 W. Mendenhall
Bozeman, MT 59715
406.586.1500

Yellowstone Traditions
PO Box 1933
Bozeman, MT 59771
406.587.0968

Rustic Furniture and Design Galleries

American West Gallery
520 4th St.
PO Box 3130
Ketchum, ID 83340
208.726.1333

Black Bass Antiques
PO Box 788
Main St.
Bolton Landing, NY 12814
518.644.2389

Chocolay River Trading Company
Pam Gilmore
2210 US 41 S.
Marquette, MI 49855
906.249.2782

Fighting Bear Antiques
PO Box 3790
375 South Cache Dr.
Jackson, WY 83001
307.733.2669

High Country Designs
PO Box 5656
720 Main St.
Frisco, CO 80443
970.668.0107

Ralph Kylloe Gallery
PO Box 669
Lake George, NY 12845
518.696.4100

Ross Bros. Gallery
28 N. Maple St.
Florence, MA. 01062
413.586.3875

The Rustic Cottage
4938 Rt. 52
Jeffersonville, NY 12748
845.482.4123

Sagebrush Interiors and Gallery
661 Sun Valley Rd.
PO Box 10014
Ketchum, ID 83340
208.726.9662

Furniture Builders

Lester Santos
2102 Southfork St.
Cody, WY 82414
307.527.7972